Grizzly Bears

NATURE'S PREDATORS

Eleanor J. Hall

KidHaven Press

KidHaven Press, an imprint of Gale Group, Inc.
P.O. Box 289009, San Diego, CA 92198-9009

Library of Congress Cataloging-in-Publication Data
Hall, Eleanor J.
    Grizzly bears / by Eleanor J. Hall.
       p. cm.—(Nature's predators)
    Includes bibliographical references (p.).
    ISBN 0-7377-0941-3 (hardback : alk. paper)
    1. Grizzly bear—Juvenile literature. [1. Grizzly bear. 2. Bears.]
I. Title. II. Series.
    QL737.C27 H357 2002
    599.784—dc21

   2001001539

Copyright 2002 by KidHaven Press, an imprint of Gale Group, Inc.
P. O. Box 289009, San Diego, CA 92198-9009

Contents

Chapter 1

Giants of the Wilderness

Grizzly bears have a well-deserved reputation as one of nature's largest and most feared **predators.** In the distant past, hunters were so amazed at the strength and courage of these powerful animals, they portrayed them in folktales as sacred beings with magical powers. In recent times scientists have challenged many of the old beliefs about grizzly bears. Some scientists even risk their lives studying and photographing them in the wilderness. As a result, much more accurate information about these gigantic predators is available today.

Horrible Bear of the North

Scientists classify all living things into groups called **species.** Members of a species share a set of physical characteristics unlike those of other groups. Each species has a scientific name taken from Latin. The scientific name for grizzly bears is ***Ursus arctos horribilis,*** meaning "horrible bear of the north."

Because scientific names are usually long and hard to pronounce, species always have common names as well, sometimes more than one. Grizzly bears get their name from the coarse outer hairs on their fur. These hairs (called guard hairs) are often tipped with gray or silver, giving the bears an old or grizzled appearance. Grizzly bears are sometimes called **silvertips** for the same reason. Although their inner coat varies in color from blond to almost black, they are also known as brown bears.

Today grizzly bears live in Russia, Canada, and the American states of Idaho, Montana, Wyoming, and Alaska. Brown bears that live along the coastal areas of Alaska are much larger than those that live in the inland mountains and forests. Except for size, however, these giant bears look and act the same as their smaller grizzly bear cousins.

Grizzly Bears Are Omnivores

Because grizzly bears eat both meat and plants, scientists classify them as **omnivores.** This is a Latin term meaning "to eat everything." Grizzly bears differ from most large predators in that meat makes up only a small part of their diet. Eighty to ninety percent of the food they eat

Grizzly bears get their name from the coarse, gray hair on their fur.

comes from plants such as grasses, bulbs, pine nuts, flowers, and berries.

Nevertheless, meat is important in a grizzly's diet because it supplies necessary fat and **protein.** Grizzly bears get meat from several sources. They prey on grazing animals such as deer, elk, caribou, and moose. They also eat **carrion,** animals that have died from other causes. In addition, grizzly bears hunt rodents such as mice, gophers, ground squirrels, and marmots (a type of groundhog). They

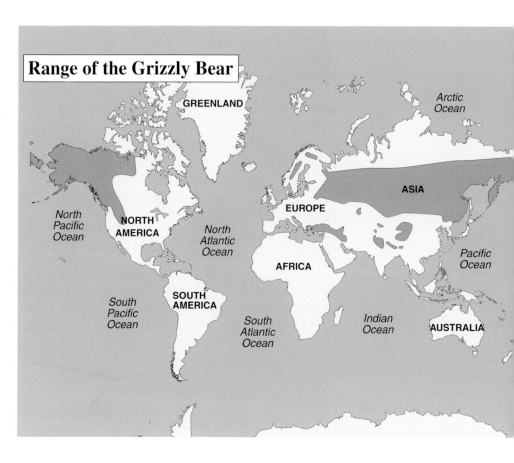

Range of the Grizzly Bear

catch fish whenever possible, and they are fond of ants, moths, and other insects.

Being omnivorous is highly beneficial for grizzly bears. Because of their great size, they must eat large amounts of food during the summer and fall in order to survive the winter. By having many food sources to rely upon, grizzly bears rarely go hungry.

The hardest part of being an omnivore is learning how to find and make use of a wide variety of foods. For instance, stalking and killing an elk requires a different set of skills than catching a mouse or a marmot. Fortunately, nature has equipped grizzly bears with numerous skills and traits to help them find and digest many different kinds of foods.

Grizzly Bears Are Well Equipped

The most visible characteristic of grizzly bears is their enormous size. On the average, male grizzlies measure six to seven feet long from nose to tail. When standing on all four feet, they are about three and a half feet tall at the shoulder. Their average weight varies from three hundred to eight hundred pounds. Of course, the size and weight of individual bears varies greatly. Males are always larger than females, sometimes twice as large. The amount and kinds of food a bear eats also make a difference.

Other features that identify a grizzly bear are a round head, small rounded ears, and a face that slopes downward toward the nose. Another identifying mark is a large hump on the bear's upper back, just behind its head. This hump is formed by the muscles of its front legs.

Large feet with five toes and thick pads give grizzly bears a solid foundation for walking and running. When they walk, grizzly bears place their feet flatly upon the ground just as humans do. This method of walking enables grizzly bears to stand erect and walk on their hind legs for short distances.

Standing erect is especially useful for predators because it allows them to see farther and to catch scents they might miss closer to the ground. When grizzlies run or charge, however, they get down on all fours. This more natural position enables them to move with amazing speed in spite of their great size.

Of course, it is not size and strength alone that makes grizzly bears fierce predators. A grizzly's huge paws are equipped with long, slightly curved claws, five on each paw. Claws on the front paws measure from three to five inches long while those on the back paws are slightly shorter. Claws serve both as weapons to kill **prey** and as tools to dig up plants and build winter dens.

Another prominent grizzly bear feature is a mouthful of sharp teeth. Long canine teeth and sharp incisors at the front of a bear's mouth are used for killing ani-

Standing up on its hind legs allows a grizzly to see farther.

A grizzly's claws can be used both as weapons and tools.

mals and tearing flesh. Broad jaw teeth with jagged edges serve as grinders for chewing up meat and tough plant fibers.

Another extremely valuable asset for hunting is a keen sense of smell. If the wind is blowing the right way, a grizzly can catch the scent of prey from a mile away. Although their hearing is very good, their eyesight is no better than that of humans.

Grizzly Bears Are Hibernators

During the winter grizzly bears keep warm and save energy by **hibernating.** To hibernate

A grizzly's teeth are good for chewing tough plants and for hunting.

means to sleep through the winter in a den of some sort. A den may be a natural place such as a cave or a hollow tree. Sometimes grizzly bears dig their own dens and line them with brush and small tree limbs for warmth and comfort.

During hibernation a bear's heartbeat and other bodily functions slow down. These changes are so extensive that a bear does not need to eat or drink for three or four months at a time. Instead, it survives off **nutrients** from the food it ate during the summer and fall. Its thick fur coat keeps it from freezing while it sleeps.

Hibernation is essential for grizzly bears. Few, if any, would survive if they had to hunt for food all winter. Hibernation is also the time when grizzly bear cubs are born inside their mothers' snug dens. Hibernation has a downside, however. A bear must be reasonably fat and healthy when it goes into its den, or it may not survive to see another spring.

Getting ready for hibernation means constantly being on the move, searching for food from spring until late fall. Eating a certain amount of meat is a vital part of this preparation. Therefore, at various times during the feeding season, grizzlies hunt live animals.

Chapter 2

Solitary Hunters

G rizzly bears hunt alone rather than in packs. Each bear has its own home range that may overlap those of other bears. If bears happen to meet in overlapping ranges, the dominant or most powerful bear usually chases the others away. However, when food is plentiful, several bears may **forage** for food in the same area.

In their wilderness habitats, grizzly bears are at the top of the **food chain.** This means they hunt other animals, but no other animals hunt them. In spite of their ferociousness, however, grizzlies are not exceptionally skillful at hunting large prey. Although they can run very swiftly, most of the big animals they hunt are able to out-run them if they get a head start.

When describing the hunting techniques of grizzly bears, **naturalists** call them opportunists. If an opportunity comes along to make a big kill, they will

Grizzlies usually hunt alone, but if food is plentiful, several grizzlies may hunt in the same area.

take it, providing they are hungry at the time. Otherwise, bears conserve their energy by going after prey that requires less effort to catch and kill, such as the newborn calves of elk and moose.

Hunting Calves

Moose are the largest members of the deer family. They generally live alone or in small, widely scattered groups. Elk, also members of the deer family, travel together in large herds. Because elk are easier to find and kill, grizzlies hunt them more often than moose.

Elk spend their summers grazing in lofty mountain valleys and meadows. In winter they **migrate** to lower elevations where it is warmer. Early in the spring, many elk cows give birth to calves, which they hide from predators in shrubs and tall grasses. Using their powerful sense of smell, hungry grizzly bears hurry to where the elk are grazing.

Elk calves are easy prey for grizzly bears.

Not all cows have calves each year, but grizzly bears have an amazing ability to single out those who do. When it spots a likely prospect, the bear charges at the cow to drive her away. From experience, the bear knows a mother elk will not defend her calf at the expense of her own life. After the cow runs away, the bear begins to move rapidly back and forth, sniffing the ground to catch the calf's scent.

Nature writer David Peterson calls this method of hunting a deadly game of hide-and-seek that grizzlies do not always win. "If the near-scentless calf has been properly stashed by its mother and is cool enough to remain quiet," he writes, "it just might escape discovery, death, and digestion."[1] When a bear does find a calf, it quickly kills the defenseless animal by biting it in the head and neck.

Stalking Adult Animals

The opportunity for catching calves lasts only a few weeks. As the surviving calves grow older and stronger, bears are forced to pursue larger, more active prey. Even then, they conserve energy by seeking out the weakest members of the herd.

Wildlife biologist Doug Peacock observed such an incident while studying bears in Yellowstone National Park. Early one morning he saw a large grizzly bear run out of the woods toward a herd of elk. Although the elk scampered away, they didn't seem too worried. Elk are used to grizzlies, and they can usually outrun them.

For a while the bear trotted peacefully behind the elk herd as if it had no harmful intentions. Then Peacock noticed the bear was focusing its attention on a particular cow. Although Peacock could see nothing unusual about the cow, the bear evidently sensed a weakness in it. Seconds later the bear charged. When it caught up with the cow, it reared up on its hind legs and knocked her to the ground with its powerful front legs. Although the blow didn't kill the cow, the bear quickly finished her off with its claws and teeth. As Peacock watched in amazement, the bear then picked up the full-grown elk in its mouth and shook it like a cat does a mouse.

Hunting Bulls

Hunting male elk or moose (called bulls) is a different matter. Grizzlies seldom take on more than they can handle, and bulls are tough opponents. They have large antlers and sharp hooves, and some of them weigh as much (or more) than the bears themselves. About the only time a grizzly goes after a bull is when the bull is sick, disabled, or in a tight spot. For instance, bears sometimes kill bulls that are trapped in deep snow or exhausted from fighting each other during the mating season.

Surprisingly, violent encounters between grizzly bears and large prey are rare. Much more of a grizzly bear's time is taken up with foraging for plants and small animals.

Hunting Small Prey

Rodents such as mice, gophers, ground squirrels, and marmots are the small animals hunted most frequently by grizzly bears. When hunting small animals, grizzly bears use their big front paws as

A grizzly bear often hunts for smaller prey such as rodents.

hands. They don't have thumbs, but they can move each of the toes on their front feet almost like fingers. Moreover, they are able to stand upright and use their front legs as humans use their arms.

Even for a big bear, preying on tiny rodents is worthwhile because they are so numerous and easy to catch. As grizzlies dig into the ground to find bulbs and roots, they scoop up tiny rodents and gulp them down on the spot. Catching and eating marmots is not quite so easy. Marmots are large rodents measuring from one to two feet long. For protection they dig deep burrows under rocks and boulders. Hunting marmots is one activity at which grizzlies do not conserve energy. They have been known to dig enormous holes and move hundreds of pounds of rocks just to catch one marmot.

Hunting small prey has another useful purpose. It is one of the ways in which mother bears teach their cubs to hunt. Biologist Frank C. Craighead Jr. spent many years observing grizzly bears in their natural habitats. On one occasion he watched a mother bear (named Marian) while she and her cub foraged for food. "When Marian . . . located a mouse nest or excavated one," Craighead writes, "her yearling came running and she permitted him to catch and eat the mouse."[2]

Hunting Other Prey

Grizzly bears are also fond of ants and other insects. To find them, they turn over rocks, tear open rotting logs, dig in the ground, and raid

Grizzlies easily catch fish in a rushing river.

anthills. They don't stop to kill these small creatures, but simply lap them up with their tongues wherever they find them.

Grizzly bears also catch fish when they have the opportunity. They wade in shallow rivers and creeks where salmon and trout come to **spawn** (lay their eggs). Because fish swim against the current when they spawn, bears catch them easily by scooping them up with their mouths and paws. When a bear catches a fish, it carries it out of the water to eat it.

Grizzly bears are not always successful at catching prey, but when they do connect, there is little doubt about the outcome. The bear will soon be eating a meal.

Chapter 3

Feasting and Fasting

When grizzly bears are not hibernating, almost all of their time is spent eating or looking for something to eat. Although grizzlies know nothing about nutrition, they do know which foods to eat in order to stay strong and healthy. Assisted by their sensitive noses and excellent memories, they know where to look for edible plants and animals at each season of the year.

This knowledge is partly **instinctive** (inborn) and partly learned. Bear cubs stay with their mothers for two or three years, learning what to eat and where to find it. By its third year, a cub may be almost as large as its mother and already eating many pounds of food a day.

Big Bears Have Big Appetites

Adult male grizzly bears lose about 30 percent of their body weight during hibernation, and adult females lose as much as 40 percent. For example, a male bear weighing 500 pounds at the beginning of hibernation could lose 150 pounds by the time it wakes up in the spring. A female bear weighing 300 pounds could lose 120 pounds.

Grizzly bears do not store food. As soon as they emerge from their dens in the spring, they begin their annual food search all over again. It is important for them to replace the weight they lost as quickly as possible. To do this, they need to find foods high in fat and protein. Sometimes their food choices are surprising.

A few years ago, naturalists discovered that grizzly bears in the western United States eat

Grizzlies must gain a lot of weight by late fall to survive hibernation.

army cutworm moths that hide on mountain slopes during late summer and fall. The moths are easy to catch and eat. All a bear has to do is turn over rocks and perhaps dig a little. Moreover, the moths cluster together, so several of them may be eaten at one time.

The moths are so plentiful that bears feed on them for weeks at a time. Some bears devour as many as twenty thousand moths a day. Because moths are very high in fat and protein, they are an extremely important food source for grizzly bears. Fortunately, the moths appear just when bears need them most.

Preparing to Hibernate

Around the middle of August, a grizzly bear's large appetite becomes even larger in preparation for hibernation. During this active feeding period, grizzly bears may eat eighty to ninety pounds of plant and animal foods each day. Their weight gain per week may be as much as forty pounds. Because meat is a rich energy source, a bear often takes more risks in hunting big game animals than it would have done earlier in the season.

Grizzly bears that are lucky enough to live near fish spawning streams gain many pounds of their winter weight from fish alone. During the spawning season, fish are available in such great numbers that bears become very choosy. "When the salmon are at their peak," writes wildlife pho-

A grizzly can eat eighty to ninety pounds of food each day.

tographer Michio Hoshino, "the grizzlies will eat only the most nourishing portions of the fish, the head and the eggs. I witnessed many scenes in which a bear would pin down a salmon with its paw, look it over, and then release it uneaten."[3]

Grizzly Bear Table Manners

Grizzly bears are not tidy when they eat. They gulp down their food very quickly, especially meat. The threat that more aggressive bears may suddenly show up and take away their kill is always present. Therefore, when a bear kills a large animal, it drags it to a sheltered place to avoid being seen by other bears. It uses its teeth and razor-sharp claws to rip open the tough hide of its prey. Once the meat is exposed, the bear tears off huge chunks and

Bears that live near spawning streams may get most of their food from fish.

swallows them with very little chewing. It also removes and eats the liver and other organs.

For a single bear or a mother with cubs, a good-sized elk will supply food for several days. Therefore, when a bear has eaten all it can hold, it digs a hole and pushes the carcass into it. Then it covers the remains with dirt, grass, leaves, and branches. For several days afterward, the bear remains nearby to finish eating its kill and to protect it from other bears.

If confronted by another bear before it can hide its kill, a large aggressive bear will drive the other bear away. A less powerful bear may back off to avoid injury and allow the intruder to take over. Sometimes the displaced bear hangs around on the fringes, waiting for the big bear to finish eating. Smaller predators such as coyotes, foxes, and even wolves may be waiting, too. By the time all the predators have finished, there is nothing left of the prey but bones and a few scraps of hide.

Sharing Food

For a long time, bears were thought to eat alone as well as hunt alone. The idea that such ferocious animals shared food or ate together was

A grizzly does not chew its food thoroughly.

Wolves and other predators sometimes try to eat grizzlies' prey.

considered highly unlikely. When naturalists began studying grizzly bears in the wild, however, they frequently observed several bears feeding peacefully at the same place.

Communal eating seems to happen only when there is plenty of food to go around. For example, twenty-three bears were observed eating army cutworm moths at the same time and place. Even more surprising, bears of all ages and both sexes were present—even mothers with cubs. Sometimes two or more grizzly bears will share the carcass of a large animal that has died of natural causes, such as a bison.

Nevertheless, a large food supply doesn't always result in sharing. Dominant grizzly bears have been known to chase lesser bears away from berry patches loaded with enough berries to feed dozens of bears. Before attempting to share food, therefore, less powerful bears always approach a feeding site very carefully.

As winter approaches, the frantic search for food comes to an end. After stuffing themselves for weeks, grizzly bears stop eating and go off to prepare a den for the winter. As the days grow cooler and shorter, bears become sluggish and drowsy. Shortly after the first snow begins to fall, grizzly bears close themselves inside their dens. Eventually the dens will be completely hidden under several feet of snow.

Adult bears hibernate by themselves, but mothers with young cubs curl up together where nothing can harm them—at least for a while. Grizzly bears have only a few enemies, but those few are very dangerous ones.

Chapter 4

Grizzly Foes and Woes

Grizzly bears have few challengers in their own habitats. Adult elk, moose, and bison fight back when attacked by grizzly bears, but none of them ever starts a fight. Because they are herbivores (plant eaters) they have no reason to risk their lives attacking grizzlies. The only animals in the wild that pose a threat to adult grizzly bears are other grizzlies. However, a few smaller animals prey on grizzly bear cubs when they get a chance.

Animal Predators

Mountain lions and bobcats have been known to kill grizzly bear cubs, but the greatest threat comes from wolves, which hunt in packs. Wolves try to separate a mother from her cubs. Some of them charge at the mother to distract her while others rush in and grab a cub. Any predator that attacks a mother grizzly is taking a big chance, however. Grizzly bear mothers will fight anything that threatens their cubs—even other grizzly bears.

For reasons that are not clearly understood by naturalists, male grizzlies kill and eat cubs. Mothers do their very best to avoid male bears, but if threatened by them, they will fight to the death. Knowing that angry mothers can inflict serious injury on them, large males usually run away. But not always.

If a male bear is intent on getting a cub, it usually tries to snatch one when the mother is busy hunting or catching fish. Sometimes it tricks the mother. While she is chasing the male bear away, it suddenly doubles back and grabs

The only wild animal that is a threat to a grizzly bear is another grizzly.

one of her unprotected cubs. Male bears that are really hungry will sometimes kill the mother bear and then get the cubs.

Nevertheless, the damage done to grizzly bears by themselves and other animals is trivial compared to that done by human beings. By far, people are the greatest enemies of grizzly bears.

People and Bears

Grizzly bears once roamed freely over the western half of North America from Canada to Mexico. With no natural enemies to keep them in check, grizzly bear populations numbered in the hundreds of thousands. Native hunters sometimes killed them, but with only spears for weapons, they did not greatly reduce the bear population.

The first Europeans to arrive in North America settled in the eastern part of the continent where there were no grizzly bears. As hunters and explorers began to push westward, Indians told them stories about giant bears that lived farther west. Such stories were not widely believed until explorers Meriwether Lewis and William Clark actually saw them and described them in their journals.

At the time of the Lewis and Clark Expedition in the early 1800s, naturalists estimate that about 100,000 grizzly bears lived in the western part of America. As the West was settled, grizzly bear numbers decreased rapidly. Today the grizzly bear population in the United States is less than a thousand. The largest concentrations are in

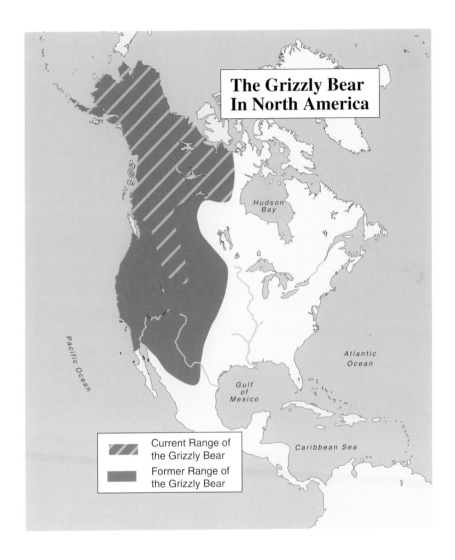

The Grizzly Bear In North America

Hudson Bay

Pacific Ocean

Atlantic Ocean

Gulf of Mexico

Caribbean Sea

Current Range of
the Grizzly Bear

Former Range of
the Grizzly Bear

Yellowstone National Park, Wyoming, and Glacier National Park, Montana. A few grizzlies still survive in parts of Idaho and Washington. The majority of grizzly bears in North America, around fifty thousand, live in Canada and Alaska.

The drastic decrease in grizzly bears, particularly those south of Canada, is due to many factors. Two very important ones are loss of habitat (living space) and public attitudes toward bears.

Loss of Habitat

Grizzly bears and human beings are able to get along fairly well as long as they both have plenty of space. Major problems begin when bears and people try to occupy the same habitat. In the early days, grizzlies could hold their own, but the balance of power changed when swarms of people with guns and other deadly weapons moved into bear country.

Grizzly bears need lots of space to thrive.

This situation did not end after America was settled. In fact, it still goes on today. Modern machinery makes it possible for housing developments and vacation resorts to be built in out-of-the-way places. Industrial development such as oil drilling and mining for minerals has expanded into former wilderness areas. In the meantime, grizzly bears are being pushed into smaller and smaller areas where they are unable to find enough food.

Whether humans and the remaining grizzlies will be able to live peaceably with each other in the future depends very much on public attitudes toward bears.

Public Attitudes Toward Bears

On the western frontier, most settlers hated grizzly bears. Rampaging bears killed domestic animals on which settlers depended, destroyed property, and sometimes killed people. As a result, grizzlies were wiped out by dozens at a time. Hundreds more were driven away from their traditional hunting grounds.

Decades later, when bears were no longer a threat to most people, attitudes changed. Bears were pictured in children's books as cuddly creatures. Teddy bears became a favorite toy for children. Fascination with real bears soon followed. During the mid-1900s, bears were the center of attention at many national parks in North America.

Attracted by the scent of food, bears came directly into campgrounds to beg or steal food. They stood along the roadsides while people handed food to them out of car windows. Some visitors even got out of their cars to feed them. Park officials allowed bears to eat garbage from the park dumps, and bleachers were set up at the dumps where people could watch.

In the wild, grizzly bears avoid trouble if at all possible. They run away from people or warn them away with growls and fake charges. However, as park visitors continued to treat bears more like large pets than wild animals, bears soon lost their fear of people. They also became accustomed to eating garbage instead of hunting and foraging in their

Grizzlies and people need to stay at a safe distance from each other.

own habitats. Tragedy followed in 1967 at Yosemite National Park, California. Two young women sleeping in different campgrounds were killed on the same night by two grizzly bears that had become accustomed to stalking campgrounds for food.

After these tragic events, park policies began to change. Visitors were no longer allowed to feed bears. Garbage dumps were closed, and bears that showed no fear of humans were either killed or moved to remote places in the parks. Many of the displaced bears, now addicted to garbage, quickly found their way back to the campgrounds. Years passed before naturalists were able to force park bears back into their own territories.

Protecting Both Bears and the Public

Today naturalists and other people interested in saving grizzly bears have formed organizations to teach people and bears how to get along without killing or hurting one another. For example, the Wind River Bear Institute in Utah helps people who live in bear country deal peaceably with problem grizzlies. The institute was founded by wildlife biologist Carrie Hunt. When Hunt and her assistants deal with a troublesome bear, they first trap and tranquilize the bear. Then they put a radio collar on it to track its movements. As long as the bear stays away from human settlements, it is left alone. If it comes back, rubber bullets and noise-making shells are fired at it. Hunt also uses trained dogs on leashes to frighten bears away.

Grizzly bears that become accustomed to human food may lose their fear of people.

None of these measures injure the bear. As Hunt explains it, "Basically, we are teaching them that we are the dominant bears and they cannot enter our personal space. Bears readily understand the concept of personal space. That's how they get along out in the wild."[4] Hunt also works with the people involved, advising them on how to keep from attracting bears to their homes in the first place.

Hunt's organization is just one of many bear-protection organizations in North America today. Although the work of each organization differs somewhat from that of others, they all have a common goal—to make it possible for humans and the remaining North American grizzly bears to live peacefully together.

Notes

1. David Peterson, *Ghost Grizzlies: Does the Great Bear Still Haunt Colorado?* New York: Henry Holt, 1995, p. 182.

2. Frank C. Craighead Jr., *Track of the Grizzly.* San Francisco: Sierra Club Books, 1982, p. 89.

3. Michio Hoshino, *Grizzly.* San Francisco: Chronicle Books, 1987, p. 41.

4. Quoted in Ben Long, "Respecting Predators in Our Changing West," *Defenders,* Winter 2000/2001, p. 15.

Glossary

carrion: Carcasses of dead animals.

food chain: A sequence of animals that feed on one another. Those at the bottom of the food chain are eaten by more powerful animals, who are eaten by still more powerful animals, and on up to the top. Grizzly bears are at the top of the food chain in areas where they live. They eat other animals, but no other animals eat them.

forage: To wander about searching for food. Grizzly bears forage in forests and meadows for plants and small animals.

hibernation: A state of deep sleep that some animals enter during the winter. All of their body processes slow down, and they live off the nutrients from the food they ate during the summer and fall. Grizzly bears hibernate from late fall to spring.

instinct: Behaviors that are inborn rather than learned.

migrate: To move from one place to another seasonally. Elk migrate each year from summer to winter feeding grounds.

naturalist: A scientist who specializes in the study of nature.

nutrients: Vitamins, minerals, and other substances in food that are essential for maintaining healthy bodies.

omnivore: An animal that eats both plants and meat. Omnivore comes from the Latin language: *omni* meaning "all" and *vore* meaning "to eat."

predator: An animal that kills and eats other animals.

prey: An animal that is killed and eaten by predators.

protein: Nutrients that are essential for growth and healthy bodies. Meat is an excellent source of protein.

silvertip: A nickname for grizzly bears that comes from the silvery tips on their fur.

spawn: An instinct in certain kinds of fish (such as salmon and trout) to travel upstream in rivers and creeks to lay their eggs. Spawning fish are a favorite food of grizzly bears.

species: A group of living things (both animals and plants) that share certain characteristics different from those of other groups.

***Ursus arctos horribilis*:** The scientific name for grizzly bears meaning "horrible bear of the north." *Ursus* is Latin for "bear," *arctos* means "north," and *horribilis* means "horrible" or "terrible."

For Further Exploration

Books

Gary Brown, *The Great Bear Almanac*. New York: Lyons Press, 1993.
A valuable source of information about all kinds of bears. It contains charts, drawings, and photographs as well as text. The author is a highly respected bear management specialist who worked for the National Park Service for many years.

———, *Outwitting Bears*. New York: Lyons Press, 2001.
A short, readable book about bear safety when camping or hiking in bear country. It also contains general information about bears and their habits.

Robert H. Busch, *The Grizzly Almanac*. New York: Lyons Press, 2000.
An excellent reference book about grizzly bears. Contents include grizzly bear history, biology, social behavior, and the problems faced by grizzly bears today. The book is enhanced with many full-color photographs.

Charles W. Chapman, *The Boy Who Loved Bears: A Pawnee Folktale*. Danbury, CT: Childrens Press, 1995.
Using his own drawings, the author retells an Indian legend about the magical powers of bears. For ages five to eight.

Daniel J. Cox and Rebecca Grambo. *Bear: A Celebration of Power and Beauty.* San Francisco: Sierra Club Books, 2000. The text (written on an adult level) provides not only factual information about bears, but myths and legends about them as well. Beautiful full-color photographs of North American bears makes this an appealing book for children as well as adults.

Andy Russell, *Great Bear Adventures: True Tales from the Wild.* Stillwater, MN: Voyageur Press, 1990. A collection of tales about grizzlies and other North American bears covering the time period from Lewis and Clark to the present. Most of the tales are taken from the writings of well-known people who have had personal encounters with bears. Young children will find this book too advanced to read themselves, but many of the stories make good listening.

Gary Turbak, *Grizzly Bears.* Stillwater, MN: Voyageur Press, 1997. Written for the general reader, this well-illustrated book provides an excellent introduction to grizzly bears for young and old alike.

Art Wolfe, *Bears: Their Life and Behavior.* New York: Crown, 1992. Although this book is written for adults, children will appreciate the dozens of beautiful color photographs of polar bears, black bears, and grizzly bears contained in it.

Websites

Cub Den (www.nature-net.com/bears/cubden.html). A website about bears especially for children. Information on all species of bears is attractively presented. Other features, such as the sound of a bear roaring, make it an appealing site for children.

Great Grizzly Hike (www.wildrockies.org/grizhike). This website tells the story of a small group of wildlife experts who hiked grizzly bear trails in Montana and Idaho. The purpose of the hike was to learn how and where bears search for food. The site contains photographs, maps, and the daily journals of the hikers.

Vital Ground Foundation (www.vitalground.org). Grizzly bears need plenty of room if they are to survive in the wilderness. The Vital Ground Foundation is dedicated to preventing loss of bear habitat. The founders of the organization also rescue abandoned bear cubs and train them to appear in movies and television shows.

Videos

The Biggest Bears: A Musical Adventure from Alaska. Broadcast Services of Alaska/Daniel Zatz, 1993. This twenty-two-minute video about grizzly bears and other wild animals of Alaska won an Emmy Award for best children's film of 1994. Besides being beautiful and entertaining, the video delivers a sensitive environmental message. Adults will enjoy it along with children.

The Grizzlies. National Geographic Society, 1987. An outstanding video about the past, present, and future of grizzly bears. Some of today's leading experts in bear management and protection are featured. Although the sixty-minute video is not made especially for children, there are many parts of it they will enjoy. For example, animal trainer and environmentalist Doug Seus demonstrates how he trains grizzly bears to appear in movies and TV shows.

Index

Picture Credits

About the Author

Freelance writer Eleanor J. Hall is an avid traveler with a particular interest in wildlife and its preservation. She has held various jobs with the National Park Service from the Florida Everglades to an Inuit community in northern Alaska. She now makes her home base in St. Louis, Missouri. Her writing credits include curriculum guides for the National Park Service, magazine articles, children's activity columns for Woodall's RV Publications, and five previous books for Lucent Books.